MW00807799

Life in the Word

Learn to Study the Bible
Accurately and Effectively

for Grades 7–12

by
Sonya Shafer

Life in the Word: Learn to Study the Bible Accurately and Effectively
© 2010 Sonya Shafer

All rights reserved. No part of this work may be reproduced or distributed in any form by any means—graphic, electronic, or mechanical, including photocopying, recording, taping, or storing in information storage and retrieval systems—without written permission from the publisher.

Published by
Simply Charlotte Mason, LLC
P.O. Box 892
Grayson, Georgia 30017-0892
ISBN 978-1-61634-088-9

Cover design: John Shafer

www.SimplyCharlotteMason.com

Contents

How to Use this Bible Study

Resources Needed

- Bible
  You choose which version you want to use.
- Bible Reference Tools (Get one, two, or all three.)
  Study Bible—A study Bible contains outlines, background information, and notes intermingled along with the text of each book of the Bible.
  Bible Commentary—A commentary records another Bible student's comments on a particular book of the Bible or all the books of the Bible. Ask your parents and pastor to recommend a good one.
  Bible Handbook—A handbook is a collection of background information and notes, somewhat similar to those found in a study Bible, but without the Bible text included.
- *Strong's Concordance*
  Strong's Concordance is available for many versions of the Bible. You can find it as a printed book, as software, or on Web sites like http://blueletterbible.org and http://biblos.com.

How It Works

Each chapter in this book will walk you through a different type of Bible study. You will learn how to perform a
Book Study—Become familiar with one book of the Bible.
Word Study—Discover what a particular word means and what God says about it.
Topical Study—Investigate what the Bible says about a certain topic.
Doctrine Study—Collect and organize doctrinal truths throughout Scripture.
Narrative Study—Make Biblical accounts come alive in your mind.
Character Study—Get to know a Bible character as a real person.
Inductive Study—Combine several study methods to dig deeper into a passage.

Just follow the simple step by step instructions in each chapter. Most study methods are repeated in another chapter to help you gain confidence in performing that type of study. Once you complete all of these studies, you can use the same step by step instructions to perform other studies on your own.

Your Schedule

Each chapter is divided into shorter lessons. You should be able to complete one lesson in one sitting. Wait at least a day before tackling the next lesson. Sure, you could complete all the lessons in a chapter in one day, but you would miss the benefits of having time to meditate on what you are studying. Spreading out your study over several days or weeks gives you time to ponder, contemplate, and consider truth rather than rushing through the study just to get it done. So take your time.

Chapter 1
Book Study of James

Let's start out by doing a Book Study. In a Book Study you focus on one book of the Bible. You'll be completing these steps in your Book Study:

1. Read through the entire book, watching for its background and purpose.

2. Read through each chapter and summarize it.

3. State the book's main theme, outline the book, and summarize it as an acrostic.

Lesson 1

For this Book Study, you'll be focusing on the book of **James**. Let's dive in.

Read through the entire book, watching for its background and purpose. An easy way to remember what you are looking for is to think of an e-mail. The four important pieces of information that are displayed when you receive an e-mail in your Inbox are

To:

From:

Date:

Subject:

Those are the items you should watch for as you read through James this time. See how many of them you can find, and record them below along with the chapter and verse references where you found them.

To: _____

_____

From: _____

_____

Date: _____

Subject: _____

_____

The writer doesn't usually come right out and say, "This is my subject." Watch for clues such as, "I wanted to write to you to . . ." or a topic that comes up often or takes up a lot of verses.

Some of that background information isn't included in the book itself. Did you notice? Use your Bible reference tools to learn more about those four key items. The tools that would probably help the most would include

- A study Bible's introduction to James
- A commentary that includes James
- A Bible handbook's notes on James

Read what one or two or all three of those resources have to say, and add any extra information you find to your notes on page 7.

Ask your pastor or parents to help you find good Bible reference tools and to recommend a good commentary.

Lesson 2

The next step in doing a Book Study is to read through each chapter and summarize it.

Read through James 1, paragraph by paragraph, and summarize each paragraph in one sentence. Ask yourself, "What is this paragraph about?" and write your answer in one sentence beside its reference below. The first two are done for you as an example.

James 1:1 **James wrote this letter to the twelve scattered tribes.**

James 1:2–4 **Welcome trials because they produce maturity.**

James 1:5–8 _____

James 1:9–11 _____

James 1:12–15 _____

James 1:16–18 _____

If you are using a Bible that gives titles for various sections in the chapters, you may not just copy those titles. Read the passages, think about the passages, and come up with your own titles.

If the paragraphs are marked differently in your Bible, feel free to follow those divisions or use the ones given here.

James 1:19–21 _____

_____

_____

James 1:22–25 _____

_____

_____

James 1:26, 27 _____

_____

_____

Now do the same thing for James 2. Summarize each paragraph in one sentence.

James 2:1–7 _____

_____

_____

James 2:8–13 _____

_____

_____

James 2:14–17 _____

_____

_____

James 2:18–23 _____

_____

_____

James 2:24–26 _____

_____

_____

Lesson 3

Continue reading through each chapter of James and summarizing it.

Read James 3 and summarize each paragraph in one sentence.

James 3:1–5
_____
_____

James 3:6–12
_____
_____

James 3:13–18
_____
_____

Do the same for James 4.

James 4:1–10
_____
_____

James 4:11, 12
_____
_____

James 4:13–17
_____
_____

Lesson 4

It's time to finish the chapter-by-chapter step of your Book Study.

Read James 5 and summarize each paragraph in one sentence.

James 5:1–6
_____
_____

James 5:7–11 _____

_____

_____

James 5:12 _____

_____

_____

James 5:13–18 _____

_____

_____

James 5:19, 20 _____

_____

_____

Now read through each chapter's summary sentences and come up with one sentence that summarizes the entire chapter. Record your chapter summaries below.

James 1 _____

_____

The study done here shows you how to do an overview of a Bible book. If you want to study the Bible book more in-depth, you can do word studies, topical studies, and other inductive studies within that book. You'll learn more about those types of studies later.

James 2 _____

_____

_____

James 3 _____

_____

_____

James 4 _____

_____

_____

James 5 _____

_____

_____

Lesson 5

You're ready for the final step of your Book Study. In this lesson you will state the book's main theme, outline the book, and summarize it as an acrostic.

Read through the entire book of James again and identify the main theme of James' letter. Think of it this way: If someone asked you, "What is the book of James about?" how would you answer them?

_____

_____

_____

_____

Create an outline of the book of James. It's not that hard since you've already summarized the chapters. Put your main theme as the title of the outline and copy each chapter's summary sentence beside its corresponding Roman numeral on the outline.

Title: _____

_____

I. _____

_____

_____

II. _____

_____

_____

III. _____

_____

_____

IV. _____

_____

_____

V. _____

_____

_____

Now it's time to make your outline easy to remember. This step will take a little creativity, so have fun. Think of a five-letter key word that reminds you of the book of James. It might be a word from your main theme of the book or just a related word. Write that five-letter word, one letter per line. (We're using a five-letter word because James has five chapters. You'll see why in a minute.)

Here's an example:

J

A

M

E

S

To finish your acrostic, jot down a reminder of each chapter in order. But (here's the creative part) your summary statement or phrase should begin with the corresponding letter in the acrostic. Think of these phrases as short titles to help you remember what is in each chapter in order.

Here's an example:

Joy in trials

A real faith

Mouths beware!

Enemy of God?

Suffering, sick, and sin

Write your acrostic below.

_____

_____

_____

_____

_____

_____

_____

_____

_____

Now memorize your acrostic and explain it to your parent or teacher. If you can do that, you have a pretty good idea of what the book of James is about. Good job.

Chapter 2
Word Study on 'Faith'

Now that you know how to do a Book Study, let's do a Word Study. Here are the steps you'll complete to do a Word Study:

1. Select a word and define it in its original language.

2. Search for passages that use that particular word and summarize what they say about it.

3. Summarize your findings and determine what principles you can learn from your study.

Lesson 1

For this Word Study, let's look at "**faith**." We'll focus our study in the book of **Galatians** and find out what that book of the Bible says about faith.

Define the word in its original language. A *Strong's Concordance* is a great tool for discovering the original meaning of the words of the Bible in their original languages. Here's how to use one.

A printed Strong's Concordance is only one option for defining Bible words in their original languages. Several software and online applications are also available to help you with definitions and researching tasks. Feel free to use one of those tools if you have it handy.

1. Find the English word in the alphabetical listing just like you would look up a word in a dictionary.
2. Within that word's listing, find the Bible reference that you are studying (for example, the listings for Galatians).
3. Note the number to the right beside your selected reference.
4. Look up that number in the back of the *Strong's Concordance* to see your word's original definition. You will find both Hebrew and Greek dictionaries back there. Be sure to use the Greek word dictionary for this study, because Galatians was originally written in Greek.

"Faith" means _____

_____

_____

_____

_____

Add to this definition by looking up "faith" in a Bible dictionary, if you have one.

Search for passages that use that particular word and summarize what they say about it. Go back to the word's listing in the front of your *Strong's Concordance* to see every time the word "faith" is used **in Galatians**. Make sure you include only the verses that use that particular Greek word (or a close relation). You'll be able to tell by looking at the number beside each entry. List below the references you find, then read each passage and summarize what it says about faith.

_____

_____

_____

_____

_____

_____

_____

_____

_____

_____

_____

_____

_____

_____

_____

_____

_____

_____

_____

_____

_____

_____

_____
_____
_____
_____
_____
_____
_____
_____
_____
_____
_____
_____
_____
_____
_____
_____
_____
_____
_____
_____
_____
_____
_____
_____
_____
_____
_____
_____
_____
_____
_____

Lesson 2

Now that you've researched the occurrences of "faith" in Paul's letter to the Galatians, put together what you have learned.

Read your findings again and summarize them in a written narration. What did Paul want the believers in Galatia to know about faith?

_____

_____

_____

_____

_____

_____

_____

_____

_____

_____

_____

_____

_____

_____

_____

_____

_____

_____

_____

_____

_____

_____

_____

_____

_____

Determine what principles you can learn from your study. What do you need to remember about "faith"?

_____

_____

_____

_____

_____

_____

_____

_____

_____

_____

_____

_____

_____

_____

_____

_____

_____

_____

_____

_____

_____

_____

_____

_____

_____

_____

_____

_____

_____

_____

_____

_____

_____

Chapter 3
Topical Study on Freedom

A Topical Study takes one topic and searches the Bible to see what it says about that topic. It's a lot like a Word Study, except you aren't limited to just the one word. In a Topical Study you brainstorm related words and phrases and research those terms too, in order to get the most complete picture you can of your selected topic. You'll complete these steps for a Topical Study:

1. *Select a topic and brainstorm all the related words and phrases you can think of.*

2. *Search for passages that include those words and phrases and summarize what they say about your selected topic.*

3. *Read through your findings and summarize what the Bible says about your topic. See what principles apply to your life.*

Lesson 1

You can also narrow the focus of your Topical Study by searching in only one passage or one book of the Bible. For this study, let's focus on the book of **Galatians** and see what it says about the topic of **freedom**.

You may not find all of the words or phrases on your brainstorm list, but the longer your list, the more you may find.

Brainstorm all the related words and phrases you can think of for your topic. Here are a few to get you started. See how many more you can add.

Freedom
_____

Liberty
_____

Bondage
_____

_____

_____

Try to think of synonyms (words that mean the same) and antonyms (words that mean the opposite) of your selected topic.

_____

_____

_____

_____

Now start working your way through your list, searching for each word or phrase in the book of Galatians. Use your *Strong's Concordance*. Note the reference every time you find one of your listed words mentioned in Galatians. Write down the words and the references you find. (You'll summarize what they say in the next lesson.)

_____

_____

_____

_____

_____

_____

_____

_____

_____

_____

_____

_____

_____

_____

_____

_____

_____

_____

_____

_____

_____

_____

_____

_____

_____

You can also check the original Greek or Hebrew word that you are studying to make sure all the passages are talking about that particular word. (Page 15 will refresh your memory on how to define a word in its original language.) Sometimes the same English word is used when the original Greek might mean two different things. It would be kind of like someone studying the topic of a "trunk" in English. He could get confused if he read two articles, one about an elephant's trunk and one about a storage trunk, and thought both articles were talking about the same thing. So make sure all the passages you look up are talking about the correct Greek or Hebrew word in your selected topic list.

_____

_____

_____

_____

_____

_____

_____

_____

_____

_____

_____

_____

_____

_____

If you find that you don't know what the verse is referring to, read the verses before and after it to figure out the context. If you're still stumped, look up that passage in a Bible reference book to get more background information. A good commentary on Galatians, a study Bible's notes on Galatians, or a Bible handbooks' notes on Galatians would be good helps to read.

_____

_____

_____

_____

_____

_____

_____

_____

_____

_____

_____

_____

Lesson 2

You have your list of verses that talk about your selected topic: freedom. Now go through your list of references, read each verse, and summarize what it says about freedom. Write your summaries on pages 22 and 23.

Lesson 3

It's time to put all the information together. You've researched what the book of Galatians says about the topic of freedom. Read through your findings and summarize them in a written narration here.

<u>Freedom in Galatians</u>

_____

_____

_____

_____

_____

_____

_____

_____

_____

_____

_____

_____

_____

_____

_____

_____

_____

_____

_____

_____

_____

_____

_____
_____
_____
_____
_____
_____
_____
_____
_____
_____
_____
_____
_____
_____
_____
_____
_____
_____
_____
_____
_____
_____
_____
_____
_____
_____
_____
_____
_____
_____
_____
_____

Based on your findings, what do you need to remember about freedom in your own life?

_____

_____

_____

_____

_____

_____

_____

_____

_____

_____

_____

_____

_____

_____

_____

_____

_____

_____

_____

_____

_____

_____

_____

_____

_____

_____

_____

Chapter 4
Doctrine Study

It is a great habit to watch for doctrinal truths as you read the Bible. Scripture is full of teachings about the basic doctrines of the Christian faith, and those teachings are scattered throughout all the books of the Bible. So it is helpful to be constantly on the lookout for those teachings. If you keep an ongoing list of what you learn, you will collect quite a lot of doctrinal truth through the years that will help you stand strong against the winds of false teaching.

The ten main doctrines are

- The Bible
- God
- Jesus Christ
- The Holy Spirit
- Man
- Sin
- Salvation
- Angels
- The Church
- Future Events

Practice finding doctrinal truths by reading **Galatians 3 and 4** and looking for any statements that teach you about the ten doctrines listed in this chapter. When you find a truth, write it in that doctrine's section on the following pages and note the reference where you found it. (You will not find a doctrinal statement in every verse.) A couple of doctrinal statements are already listed to get you started.

You can make your own doctrine notebook by using a three-ring binder or spiral notebook and creating a section for each of the ten doctrines listed in this lesson. As you discover doctrinal truths in your reading, jot them down in the appropriate sections.

If you would like a doctrine notebook that is already printed and ready to use for many years, you will find Discovering Doctrine *at http://simplycharlottemason.com/books/discovering-doctrine-personal-bible-study*

The Bible

_____

_____

_____

_____

_____

_____

_____

_____

God

_____

_____

_____

_____

_____

_____

_____

_____

_____

_____

_____

_____

Jesus Christ

Born of a woman, born under the law to redeem those who

were under the law (Gal. 4:4).

_____

_____

_____

_____

_____

_____

_____

_____

_____

_____

Remember that you are looking for statements of truth about each area of doctrine. Statements that direct you in your Christian walk are profitable too, but don't need to be recorded as doctrines. For example, Galatians 5:24 says, "And they that are Christ's have crucified the flesh with the affections and lusts" (KJV). That verse describes what a follower of Christ should do, but it does not tell us about Christ Himself, so it wouldn't need to be recorded as a doctrinal statement.

Holy Spirit

_____

_____

_____

_____

_____

_____

_____

_____

_____

_____

_____

Man

_____

_____

_____

_____

_____

_____

_____

_____

_____

_____

_____

_____

_____

_____

Sin

_____
_____
_____
_____
_____
_____
_____
_____
_____
_____
_____
_____

Salvation

No one is justified before God by the law (Gal. 3:11).

When we are redeemed we receive adoption as sons (Gal. 4:5).

_____
_____
_____
_____
_____
_____
_____
_____
_____
_____
_____

Angels

_____
_____
_____
_____
_____
_____
_____
_____
_____
_____
_____

The Church

_____
_____
_____
_____
_____
_____
_____
_____
_____
_____
_____
_____
_____

Future Events

_____

_____

_____

_____

_____

_____

_____

_____

_____

_____

_____

_____

Any time you are reading the Bible—whether for personal devotions, assigned passages, listening to a sermon, family devotions, or other times—try to keep an eye out for doctrinal truths and record them in your doctrine notebook. This is a fascinating and beneficial study that can continue through the rest of your life.

Chapter 5
Narrative Study of Acts 17

Narrative Studies are for passages that tell a story or give an account of an event that happened. You'll complete these steps in a Narrative Study:

1. *Read the passage and create a storyboard or write scene descriptions to show Who, What, Where, and When the account happened.*

2. *Read the passage and any Bible reference books to help you determine Why and How the account's events happened.*

3. *Record any principles the account teaches.*

Lesson 1

For this Narrative Study, let's read the account of Paul at Thessalonica. You'll find it in **Acts 17:1–14**.

Read the passage and create a storyboard or write scene descriptions to show Who, What, Where, and When the account happened.

Here are some scene suggestions to help you get started. You can use these scene divisions or come up with your own.

Scene 1: Paul in the Synagogue
Scene 2: Different Reactions
Scene 3: Jason's House
Scene 4: Reception at Berea
Scene 5: Trouble at Berea

Record your scene titles, then write your scene descriptions on pages 34 and 35, or draw your storyboards on pages 36 and 37.

_____

_____

_____

_____

_____

A storyboard is somewhat like a comic strip. You can use it to illustrate each scene as the action unfolds in the passage. If you would rather write than draw, divide the account into scenes and describe the action in each one.

Scene Descriptions

_____

_____

_____

_____

_____

_____

_____

_____

_____

_____

_____

_____

_____

_____

_____

_____

_____

_____

_____

_____

_____

_____

_____

_____

_____

_____

_____

Scene Storyboards (Use as many as you need.)

Lesson 2

Continue your Narrative Study by looking for the Why and How of the event.

Read the passage and any Bible reference books to help you determine Why and How the account's events happened. Look for answers to the questions listed below.

Remember, if you can't find the answer to a question in the passage itself, check a Bible reference book such as a trusted commentary, a study Bible, or a Bible handbook.

How and Why Questions and Answers

Why did the unbelieving Jews cause this trouble?

_____

_____

_____

_____

_____

_____

_____

_____

_____

_____

Why did they accuse Paul and his companions of turning the world upside down?

_____

_____

_____

_____

_____

_____

_____

_____

_____

_____

_____

How did the custom of taking "security" money work?

_____

_____

_____

_____

_____

_____

_____

_____

_____

_____

_____

It's important to take the Scripture passage at "face value." Don't try to read into it some mysterious message. It's not intended to be mysterious and mystical. For example, suppose you received an e-mail from your friend who lives in another town. The e-mail read, "Mom says I can come for a visit next week. I'll be at your house Tuesday around supper time." Would you start looking for hidden meanings, trying to count the letters in "Friday" and come up with an alternate date or something like that? No. Take the writing at face value. What does it say? Your friend is coming for a visit and will arrive next Tuesday around supper time. What does it mean? Your friend will arrive next Tuesday about 6:00 (or whenever you usually have supper). How does the message apply to you? Party time! Get your homework done so you don't have to mess with it while your friend is here. Oh, and clean your room before Tuesday evening. . . .

How did the Bereans contrast with the Thessalonians?

_____

_____

_____

_____

_____

_____

_____

_____

_____

_____

_____

_____

_____

_____

_____

Record any principles the account teaches. What can you learn about sharing the gospel? about responding to troublemakers? about determining whether teachers are telling truth?

. . . It's the same with Scripture. Follow the same simple questions: What does it say? What does it mean? How does it apply to me?

_____

_____

_____

_____

_____

_____

_____

_____

_____

_____

_____

_____

_____

_____

_____

_____

_____

_____

_____

_____

_____

_____

_____

_____

Chapter 6

Book Study of 2 Thessalonians

It's time to do another Book Study. Remember, in a Book Study you focus on becoming familiar with one book of the Bible. You'll be completing these steps in your Book Study:

1. *Read through the entire book, watching for its background and purpose.*

2. *Read through each chapter, paragraph by paragraph, and summarize it.*

3. *State the book's main theme, outline the book, and summarize it as an acrostic.*

Lesson 1

Look back at your Book Study of James on pages 7–13 for help if you need it.

For this Book Study, you'll be focusing on the book of **2 Thessalonians**. Let's see how much of this study you can do on your own.

Read through the entire book, watching for its background and purpose.

To: _____

_____

From: _____

_____

Date: _____

Subject: _____

_____

The writer doesn't usually come right out and say, "This is my subject." Watch for clues such as, "I wanted to write to you to . . ." or a topic that comes up often or takes up a lot of verses.

Use your Bible study resources to learn more about those four key items. The resources that would probably help the most would include

• A study Bible's introduction to 2 Thessalonians

• A commentary that includes 2 Thessalonians

• A Bible handbook's notes on 2 Thessalonians

Read what one or two or all three of those resources have to say, and add any extra information you find to your notes above.

Lesson 2

The next step in doing a Book Study is to read through each chapter and summarize it.

Read through 2 Thessalonians 1 and 2, paragraph by paragraph, and summarize each paragraph in one sentence.

_____

_____

_____

_____

_____

_____

_____

_____

_____

_____

_____

_____

_____

_____

_____

_____

_____

_____

_____

_____

_____

_____

_____

_____

_____

_____

_____

_____

_____

_____

_____

_____

_____

_____

_____

_____

_____

_____

Lesson 3

Continue reading through each chapter of 2 Thessalonians and summarizing it.

Read 2 Thessalonians 3 and summarize each paragraph in one sentence.

_____

_____

_____

_____

_____

_____

_____

_____

_____

_____

_____

_____

_____

_____

_____

_____

_____

_____

_____

_____

_____

_____

_____

_____

_____

_____

Lesson 4

It's time to finish your Book Study.

Read through each chapter's summary sentences and come up with one summary sentence for the entire chapter. Record your chapter summaries below.

_____

_____

_____

_____

_____

_____

_____

_____

_____

_____

Read through the entire book of 2 Thessalonians again and identify the main theme of that letter.

_____

_____

_____

_____

_____

_____

Create an outline of the book of 2 Thessalonians, using your main theme and chapter summaries.

Title: _____

_____

I. _____

_____

_____

II. _____

_____

_____

III. _____

_____

_____

Create an acrostic that will make your outline easy to remember. Since 2 Thessalonians has three chapters, think of a three-letter key word that will work and complete your acrostic.

_____

_____

_____

_____

_____

Memorize your acrostic of 2 Thessalonians and explain it to your parent or teacher.

Chapter 7
Character Study on Paul

Another great study you can do in the Bible is to study the life of a Bible character. The Lord included personal information about real people in His Word, and we can learn from them—not just their words but also what happened to them, how they responded, the struggles they had, and the victories they experienced.

You'll be completing these steps in your Character Study:

1. *Search for passages that include the person's name and summarize what you find out about him.*

2. *Search for passages in which the person describes himself or his life and summarize what you find out about him.*

3. *Read through your discoveries and determine what lessons you can learn from that person's life.*

Lesson 1

For this Character Study, let's focus on **Paul** and see what lessons we can learn from his life.

Search for your character's name in *Strong's Concordance* and record all the references that you find.

To save time, we've listed the passages for you. Use this lesson and lesson 2 to read the passages and record what you find out about Paul.

Remember that you may need to read verses before and after the ones listed in order to determine the context: who was talking, what was happening, where, and why.

Acts 13:1–12 _____

_____

_____

_____

_____

_____

_____

Acts 13:13–16 and 42, 43
_____
_____
_____
_____
_____
_____

Acts 13:44–52
_____
_____
_____
_____
_____
_____
_____

Acts 14:8–18
_____
_____
_____
_____
_____
_____

You may want to spread this lesson out over several days since there are so many passages to read about Paul.

Acts 14:19–23
_____
_____
_____
_____
_____
_____

Acts 15:1, 2, 12, 22
_____
_____
_____
_____
_____
_____

Acts 15:36–41 _____

_____

_____

_____

_____

_____

Acts 16:1–5 _____

_____

_____

_____

_____

Acts 16:6–10 _____

_____

_____

_____

_____

Acts 16:11–15 _____

_____

_____

_____

_____

Acts 16:16–40 _____

_____

_____

_____

_____

_____

Acts 17:1–9

_____

_____

_____

_____

_____

Acts 17:10–15

_____

_____

_____

_____

Acts 17:16–23

_____

_____

_____

_____

Acts 18:1–4

_____

_____

_____

_____

Acts 18:5–11

_____

_____

_____

_____

_____

Acts 18:12–17

_____

_____

_____

_____

_____

Acts 18:18–23

_____

_____

_____

_____

_____

Acts 19:1–10

_____

_____

_____

_____

_____

Acts 19:11, 12

_____

_____

_____

_____

_____

Acts 19:23—20:3

_____

_____

_____

_____

_____

Acts 20:7–12 _____

_____

_____

_____

_____

_____

_____

Lesson 2

Continue doing your research about Paul's life. Read the rest of these passages from Acts that mention Paul and record what you find out about him.

Acts 21:8–14 _____

_____

_____

_____

_____

_____

Acts 21:17–19 _____

_____

_____

_____

_____

Acts 21:26–36 _____

_____

_____

_____

_____

_____

_____

Acts 21:37—22:1

_____

_____

_____

_____

_____

Acts 22:22–29

_____

_____

_____

_____

_____

Acts 22:30—23:11

_____

_____

_____

_____

You may want to spread this lesson out over several days since there are so many passages to read about Paul.

Acts 23:12–24

_____

_____

_____

_____

_____

Acts 24:1, 10–22

_____

_____

_____

_____

_____

Acts 24:24–26

Acts 24:27—25:12

Acts 25:23—26:1

Acts 27:1–12

Acts 27:13–26

Acts 27:27–38

_____
_____
_____
_____
_____
_____

Acts 27:39–44

_____
_____
_____
_____
_____
_____

Acts 28:1–10

_____
_____
_____
_____
_____
_____

Acts 28:16–31

_____
_____
_____
_____
_____
_____

Lesson 3

Paul's name is also mentioned in his writings, usually in the greeting. Search for Paul's name in the rest of the New Testament (other than the book of Acts) and list those references. (Be sure to leave space between the references so you can write your findings.) Then read those verses and record what they say about Paul.

_____

_____

_____

_____

_____

_____

_____

_____

_____

_____

_____

_____

_____

_____

_____

_____

_____

_____

_____

_____

_____

_____

_____

_____

_____

_____

_____

_____

_____

_____

_____

_____

_____

_____

_____

_____

_____

_____

_____

_____

_____

_____

_____

_____

_____

_____

_____

_____

_____

_____

_____

_____

_____

_____

_____

_____

_____

_____

_____

_____

_____

Lesson 4

A few other passages talk about Paul but don't mention him by that name. Read these passages and record what you find out about Paul.

Acts 7:58—8:3 _____

_____

_____

_____

_____

_____

Acts 9:1–19 _____   *Remember that Acts*
                                                                        13:9 explains Paul
_____   *was also called Saul.*

_____

_____

_____

_____

_____

_____

_____

_____

Acts 9:20–22 _____

_____

_____

_____

_____

_____

Acts 9:23–25 _____

_____

_____

_____

_____

_____

Acts 9:26–30 _____

_____

_____

_____

_____

_____

Acts 11:25, 26 _____

_____

_____

_____

_____

_____

Acts 11:30 _____

_____

_____

_____

_____

_____

Acts 13:1–3 _____

Notice how Acts 13:1–3 lays the foundation for Paul's travels that you already recorded in lessons 1 and 2.

_____

_____

_____

_____

2 Corinthians 11:22—12:10 _____

_____

_____

_____

_____

_____

_____

Philippians 3:4–7 _____

_____

_____

_____

_____

_____

_____

Lesson 5

You have researched a lot of verses about Paul. Now it is time to summarize your findings.

Do you see any repeated descriptions or events? Try to consolidate what you can and summarize your main discoveries about Paul's life.

_____

_____

_____

_____

_____

_____

Sometimes it's helpful to ask yourself, How would I describe Paul to a person who didn't know about him?

_____

_____

_____

_____

_____

_____

_____

_____

_____

_____

_____

_____

_____

_____

_____

_____

_____

_____

_____

_____

_____

_____

_____

_____

_____

_____

_____

_____

_____

_____

_____

_____

_____

_____

_____

_____

_____

_____

_____

_____

What lessons can you learn from Paul's life—good or bad? Read your findings again and record the lessons you can learn from your Character Study on Paul.

_____

_____

_____

_____

_____

_____

_____

_____

_____

_____

_____

_____

_____

_____

_____

_____

_____

_____

_____

_____

_____

_____

_____

_____

_____

_____

_____

_____

Chapter 8
Narrative Study of Acts 18

Do you remember how to do a Narrative Study? Here are the steps to complete:

1. *Read the passage and create a storyboard or write scene descriptions to show Who, What, Where, and When the account happened.*

2. *Read the passage and any Bible reference books to help you determine Why and How the account's events happened.*

3. *Record any principles the account teaches.*

Lesson 1

This time focus your study on what happened when Paul was at Corinth. You'll find the account recorded in **Acts 18:1–18**.

If you need a reminder of how to do a storyboard or scene descriptions, look at pages 33–40.

Read the passage and create a storyboard or write scene descriptions to show Who, What, Where, and When the account happened. As you read the passage, come up with the scene divisions and titles, then take it from there.

Scene Titles
_____
_____
_____
_____
_____
_____
_____
_____
_____
_____
_____

Scene Descriptions

_____

_____

_____

_____

_____

_____

_____

_____

_____

_____

_____

_____

_____

_____

_____

_____

_____

_____

_____

_____

_____

_____

_____

_____

_____

_____

Scene Storyboards (Use as many as you need.)

Lesson 2

Complete your Narrative Study by thinking about the Why and How.

Read the passage and any Bible reference books to help you determine Why and How the account's events happened. Think about your Why and How questions and write them down first, then look for the answers to them.

Why and How Questions and Answers

_____

_____

_____

_____

_____

_____

_____

_____

_____

_____

_____

_____

_____

_____

_____

_____

_____

_____

_____

_____

_____

_____

_____

_____

_____

_____

_____

_____

_____

_____

_____

_____

_____

_____

_____

_____

_____

_____

_____

_____

_____

_____

_____

_____

_____

_____

_____

_____

_____

_____

_____

_____

_____

_____

_____

_____

_____

_____

_____

_____

Record any principles the account teaches. What can you learn from the account's events?

_____

_____

_____

_____

_____

_____

_____

_____

_____

_____

_____

_____

_____

_____

_____

_____

_____

_____

_____

_____

_____

_____

_____

_____

_____

_____

_____

_____

Chapter 9
Topical Study on Weakness

Let's see what you remember about doing a Topical Study. The steps are

1. *Select a topic and brainstorm all the related words and phrases you can think of.*

2. *Search for passages that include those words and phrases and summarize what they say about your selected topic.*

3. *Read through your findings and summarize what the Bible says about your topic. See what principles apply to your life.*

Lesson 1

For this Topical Study, focus on finding out what the book of **1 Corinthians** says about the topic of the "**weak.**"

Brainstorm all the related words and phrases you can think of.

Try to think of synonyms (words that mean the same) and antonyms (words that mean the opposite) of your selected topic.

_____

_____

_____

_____

_____

_____

_____

_____

_____

_____

_____

Search for passages that include those words and phrases and list them below. Be sure to leave space between references to record your findings later.

_____

_____

_____

_____

_____

_____

_____

_____

_____

_____

_____

_____

_____

_____

_____

_____

_____

_____

_____

_____

_____

_____

_____

_____

_____

_____

_____

_____

_____

_____

_____

_____

_____

_____

_____

_____

_____

_____

_____

_____

_____

_____

_____

_____

_____

_____

_____

_____

_____

_____

_____

Lesson 2

Read the passages you listed above and summarize what they say about your selected topic.

Lesson 3

Read through your findings and summarize what 1 Corinthians says about the "weak."

_____

_____

_____

_____

_____

_____

_____

_____

_____

_____

_____

_____

_____

_____

_____

_____

_____

_____

_____

_____

_____

_____

_____

_____

_____

_____

_____

_____

_____
_____
_____
_____
_____
_____
_____
_____
_____
_____
_____
_____
_____
_____
_____
_____
_____
_____
_____
_____
_____
_____
_____
_____
_____
_____
_____
_____
_____
_____
_____
_____

See what principles apply to your life. What do you need to remember about the "weak"?

_____

_____

_____

_____

_____

_____

_____

_____

_____

_____

_____

_____

_____

_____

_____

_____

_____

_____

_____

_____

_____

_____

_____

_____

_____

_____

_____

_____

_____

Chapter 10
Inductive Study of 2 Corinthians 4

You've already learned many Bible study skills. In an inductive study of a passage, you put all those skills together, plus add a couple of new ones. You'll be completing these steps in an inductive study:

1. *Read the passage and determine the main idea.*

2. *Define in their original language any key words in the passage that relate to the main idea.*

3. *Look for words in the passage that are repeated for emphasis and define them in their original language.*

4. *Look for any words in the passage that you don't know the definition of and research what they mean in their original language.*

5. *Look for contrasts and comparisons in the passage.*

6. *Look for cause and effect within the passage.*

7. *Look for any lists or series given in the passage.*

8. *Look for any proper names that are mentioned in the passage and learn what you can about those people or places.*

9. *Narrate the passage in your own words, incorporating your findings.*

10. *Record any personal observations from your studies.*

An inductive study is the opposite of coming to a passage with a predetermined idea already in your head and trying to make the passage fit your idea. That erroneous approach involves reading into a passage, rather than drawing out of a passage. The technical terms for those two approaches are "exegesis" (drawing out) versus "eisegesis" (reading into).

As you can see, an inductive study digs into the passage. The goal is to draw out what the passage actually says.

Lesson 1

As you learned in the Book Studies you completed, it works well to take a chapter of the Bible paragraph by paragraph. For this study, we will look at the paragraphs of **2 Corinthians 4**, one paragraph each lesson.

Read 2 Corinthians 4:1–6 and determine the **main idea**. Try to state that main idea in one sentence.

_____

_____

_____

_____

What **key words** in that passage led you to that main idea? List them here then define them in their original language. (Look up their Greek definitions in *Strong's Concordance.*)

For a reminder of how to look up a definition in Strong's, *see page 15.*

_____

_____

_____

_____

_____

_____

_____

_____

_____

_____

Read 2 Corinthians 4:1–6 again and look for any words that are **repeated** for emphasis. List them here and define them in their original language.

_____

_____

_____

_____

_____

_____

_____

_____

_____

Read 2 Corinthians 4:1–6 again and look for any words in the passage that you **don't know** the definition of. List them and look up their definitions in *Strong's*.

_____

_____

_____

_____

_____

_____

_____

_____

_____

_____

_____

If you don't find any unknown words or any lists or any of the other "Look for" steps of an inductive study, just leave that step blank and move on.

To find contrasts, look for antonyms (words that mean the opposite). Also look for the conjunction "but" to find a possible contrast in ideas. To find comparisons, look for the words "like" or "as." Sometimes those words will give away the location of a comparison.

Read 2 Corinthians 4:1–6 again and look for **contrasts and comparisons.** List below any contrasts or comparisons that you find and look up those words' definitions in *Strong's*. (For example, did you notice the contrast between light and darkness, along with their related terms, in these verses?)

_____

_____

_____

_____

_____

_____

_____

_____

_____

Read 2 Corinthians 4:1–6 again and look for **cause and effect.** Do you see any words like "therefore" or "wherefore"? Those words will identify a cause and effect for you to summarize.

_____

_____

_____

_____

_____

_____

_____

_____

_____

_____

The concept given before the "therefore" or "wherefore" is the cause. The concept give after one of those words is the effect.

Read 2 Corinthians 4:1–6 again and look for any **lists or series.** Write the words of the list or series below and define them in *Strong's.*

_____

_____

_____

_____

_____

_____

_____

_____

_____

_____

_____

_____

_____

Read 2 Corinthians 4:1–6 again and look for any **proper names** that are mentioned. Write them below, then check a Bible reference book to learn what you can about those people or places.

A Bible commentary or handbook would be a good place to find out more about proper names. Or you can follow the same steps you learned in doing a Character Study.

_____

_____

_____

_____

_____

_____

_____

Now, read 2 Corinthians 4:1–6 again and **narrate** the passage in your own words, incorporating your findings.

_____

_____

_____

_____

_____

_____

_____

After you have studied and narrated the passage, read what another Bible student says about it in a reliable commentary.

_____

_____

_____

_____

_____

_____

_____

_____

_____

Record any personal observations from your studies. Did any of the verses challenge you to change your thinking or behavior? Did any part of the passage remind you of other Scripture verses? Did you have any "ah-ha" moments?

_____

_____

_____

_____

_____

_____

_____

_____

_____

_____

_____

_____

_____

Notice how in an inductive study, you look at the whole, then study the parts, then put it all together as a whole again.

Lesson 2

How much do you recall about 2 Corinthians 4:1–6? Probably quite a bit, because you took the time to read it several times and dig deeply into what it says. Let's study the next paragraph of 2 Corinthians 4 today.

Read 2 Corinthians 4:7–12 and determine the **main idea**. Try to state that main idea in one sentence.

_____

_____

_____

_____

_____

_____

What **key words** in that passage led you to that main idea? List them here then define them in their original language.

_____

_____

_____

_____

_____

Sometimes it helps to print out a copy of the passage and mark repeated words or key words on the paper.

_____

_____

_____

_____

Read 2 Corinthians 4:7–12 again and look for any words that are **repeated** for emphasis. List them here and define them in their original language.

_____

_____

_____

_____

_____

_____

_____

Remember, if you don't find anything for one of the "Look for" steps of an inductive study, just leave that step blank and move on.

_____

_____

Read 2 Corinthians 4:7–12 again and look for any words in the passage that you **don't know** the definition of. List them and look up their definitions in *Strong's*.

_____

_____

_____

_____

_____

Read 2 Corinthians 4:7–12 again and look for **contrasts and comparisons.** List below any contrasts or comparisons that you find and look up those words' definitions in *Strong's*.

_____

_____

_____

_____

_____

_____

_____

_____

_____

_____

_____

Read 2 Corinthians 4:7–12 again and look for **cause and effect.** Do you see any words like "therefore" or "wherefore"? Those words will identify a cause and effect for you to summarize below.

_____

_____

_____

_____

_____

_____

_____

_____

_____

_____

_____

_____

Read 2 Corinthians 4:7–12 again and look for any **lists or series.** Write the words of the list or series below and define them in *Strong's.*

_____

_____

_____

_____

_____

_____

_____

_____

_____

_____

_____

Read 2 Corinthians 4:7–12 again and look for any **proper names** that are mentioned. Write them below, then check a Bible reference book to learn what you can about those people or places.

_____

_____

_____

_____

_____

_____

_____

_____

_____

_____

Now, read 2 Corinthians 4:7–12 again and **narrate** the passage in your own words, incorporating your findings.

_____

_____

_____

_____

_____

_____

_____

_____

_____

_____

_____

_____

_____

_____

_____

_____

_____

_____

_____

_____   *After you have stud-*
ied and narrated the
_____   *passage, read what*
another Bible student
_____   *says about it in a reli-*
able commentary.
_____

_____

_____

Record any personal observations from your studies. Did any of the verses challenge you to change your thinking or behavior? Did any part of the passage remind you of other Scripture verses? Did you have any "ah-ha" moments?

_____

_____

_____

_____

_____

_____

_____

_____

_____

_____

_____

_____

_____

_____

As you complete any Bible study, be on the alert for doctrinal truths to record in your doctrine notebook. (See page 27 for a reminder.)

Lesson 3

The more you perform an inductive study, the easier it will be to notice the different parts and narrate the whole passage. Keep practicing! Today let's do the third paragraph of the chapter.

Read 2 Corinthians 4:13–15 and determine the **main idea.** Try to state that main idea in one sentence.

_____

_____

_____

_____

What **key words** in that passage led you to that main idea? List them here then define them in their original language.

_____

_____

_____

_____

_____

_____

_____

_____

_____

_____

Read 2 Corinthians 4:13–15 again and look for words that are **repeated** for emphasis. List them here and define them in their original language.

_____

_____

_____

_____

_____

_____

_____

_____

Read 2 Corinthians 4:13–15 again and look for any words in the passage that you **don't know** the definition of. List them and look up their definitions in *Strong's*.

_____

_____

_____

_____

_____

_____

_____

_____

Remember, if you don't find anything for one of the "Look for" steps of an inductive study, just leave that step blank and move on.

Read 2 Corinthians 4:13–15 again and look for **contrasts and comparisons.** List below any contrasts or comparisons that you find and look up those words' definitions in *Strong's*.

_____

_____

_____

_____

_____

_____

_____

_____

_____

_____

_____

Read 2 Corinthians 4:13–15 again and look for **cause and effect.** Do you see any words like "therefore" or "wherefore"? Those words will identify a cause and effect for you to summarize below.

_____

_____

_____

_____

_____

_____

_____

_____

_____

_____

Read 2 Corinthians 4:13–15 again and look for any **lists or series.** Write the words of the list or series below and define them in *Strong's.*

_____

_____

_____

_____

_____

_____

_____

_____

_____

_____

_____

_____

Read 2 Corinthians 4:13–15 again and look for any **proper names** that are mentioned. Write them below, then check a Bible reference book to learn what you can about those people or places.

_____

_____

_____

_____

_____

_____

_____

_____

_____

Now, read 2 Corinthians 4:13–15 again and **narrate** the passage in your own words, incorporating your findings.

_____

_____

_____

_____

_____

_____

_____

_____

_____

_____

_____

_____

_____

_____

_____

_____

_____

After you have stud-
ied and narrated the
passage, read what
another Bible student
says about it in a reli-
able commentary.

_____

_____

_____

_____

_____

_____

_____

_____

_____

Record any personal observations from your studies. Did any of the verses challenge you to change your thinking or behavior? Did any part of the passage remind you of other Scripture verses? Did you have any "ah-ha" moments?

_____

_____

_____

_____

_____

_____

_____

_____

_____

_____

_____

_____

_____

Lesson 4

Hopefully, you feel like you know 2 Corinthians 4 pretty well to this point. Let's finish up with the final paragraph today.

Read 2 Corinthians 4:16–18 and determine the **main idea.** Try to state that main idea in one sentence.

_____

_____

_____

_____

What **key words** in that passage led you to that main idea? List them here then define them in their original language.

_____

_____

_____

_____

_____

_____

_____

_____

_____

_____

Read 2 Corinthians 4:16–18 again and look for words that are **repeated** for emphasis. List them here and define them in their original language.

_____

_____

_____

_____

_____

_____

_____

_____

Read 2 Corinthians 4:16–18 again and look for any words in the passage that you **don't know** the definition of. List them and look up their definitions in *Strong's*.

_____

_____

_____

If you would like to practice these skills more, look for Foundations in Romans. *That Bible study will guide you through an inductive study of the entire book of Romans. You can find* Foundations in Romans *at http:// simplycharlottemason. com/books/founda-tions-in-romans*

_____

_____

_____

_____

Read 2 Corinthians 4:16–18 again and look for **contrasts and comparisons.** List below any contrasts or comparisons that you find and look up those words' definitions in *Strong's*.

_____

_____

_____

_____

_____

_____

_____

_____

_____

_____

_____

Read 2 Corinthians 4:16–18 again and look for **cause and effect.** Do you see any words like "therefore" or "wherefore"? Those words will identify a cause and effect for you to summarize below.

_____

_____

_____

_____

_____

_____

_____

_____

_____

_____

Read 2 Corinthians 4:16–18 again and look for any **lists or series.** Write the words of the list or series below and define them in *Strong's*.

_____

_____

_____

_____

_____

_____

_____

_____

_____

_____

_____

_____

Read 2 Corinthians 4:16–18 again and look for any **proper names** that are mentioned. Write them below, then check a Bible reference book to learn what you can about those people or places.

_____

_____

_____

_____

_____

_____

_____

_____

_____

_____

Now, read 2 Corinthians 4:16–18 again and **narrate** the passage in your own words, incorporating your findings.

_____

_____

_____

_____

_____

_____

_____

_____

_____

_____

_____

_____

_____

_____

_____

_____

_____

_____

_____

_____

_____

_____

_____

After you have studied and narrated the passage, read what another Bible student says about it in a reliable commentary.

_____

_____

_____

_____

_____

_____

_____

_____

Record any personal observations from your studies. Did any of the verses challenge you to change your thinking or behavior? Did any part of the passage remind you of other Scripture verses? Did you have any "ah-ha" moments?

_____

_____

_____

_____

_____

Once you finish an inductive study of a chapter, you can outline the chapter like you did in the Book Study.

_____

_____

_____

Chapter 11
Character Study on Titus

Let's do another Character Study. Remember, the steps in a Character Study are

1. *Search for passages that include the person's name and summarize what you find out about him.*

2. *Search for passages in which the person describes himself or his life and summarize what you find out about him.*

3. *Read through your discoveries and determine what lessons you can learn from that person's life.*

Lesson 1

For this Character Study, see what you can find out about **Titus.**

Search in *Strong's Concordance* for passages that include the person's name and summarize what you find out about him. (Be sure to leave space between the references so you can write your findings.)

_____

_____

_____

_____

_____

_____

_____

_____

_____

_____

_____

_____

_____

_____

_____

_____

_____

_____

_____

_____

_____

_____

_____

_____

_____

_____

_____

_____

_____

_____

Lesson 2

Search for passages in which the person describes himself or his life and summarize what you find out about him.

Since we don't have any writings from Titus, check a Bible reference book and see what else you can find out about him there. You might look in a study Bible's introduction to the book of Titus (that Paul wrote to him) or in a Bible handbook's notes on Titus. Record your findings.

_____

_____

_____

_____

_____

_____

_____

_____

_____

It's time to summarize what you found out about Titus and determine what lessons you can learn from his life.

_____

_____

_____

_____

_____

_____

_____

_____

_____

_____

_____

_____

_____

_____

_____

_____

_____

_____

_____

_____

_____

_____

_____

_____

_____

_____

_____

Basic Principles of Bible Study

1. Practice "exegesis."

Seek to draw out what the Scripture passage actually says. Don't come with a predetermined idea already in your head and try to make the passage fit your idea.

2. Take Scripture at face value.

Don't try to read into Scripture some mysterious message. Ask yourself three key questions: What does it say? What does it mean? How does it apply to me?

3. Keep verses in context.

Read the verses before and after your selected passage to determine the context of who was speaking, to whom, and in what situation. You wouldn't like to be misquoted because someone pulled your words out of context; give God's Word the same respect.

4. Understand the original language.

Remember that you are dealing with words that were originally written in a different language. Look up words' definitions in their original languages in order to gain a full and accurate picture of their meanings. Use *Strong's Concordance* or another Bible study tool to help you.

5. Go from whole to parts to whole.

Read a passage for the main idea, then dig into its parts, then put it all back together again.

6. Study to obey.

God's Word is powerful, even more so if you allow it to change your life. You must determine to apply what you learn. Watch for lessons and principles that challenge you to change your thinking or behavior, then purpose to obey God's Word.